CHARITIES IN ACTION

IMPROVING HEALTHCARE

Cath Senker

www.raintreepublishers.co.uk
Visit our website to find out
more information about
Raintree books.

To order:
☎ Phone 0845 6044371
▤ Fax +44 (0) 1865 312263
▧ Email myorders@raintreepublishers.co.uk

Customers from outside the UK please telephone +44 1865 312262

Raintree is an imprint of Capstone Global Library
Limited, a company incorporated in England and
Wales having its registered office at 7 Pilgrim Street,
London, EC4V 6LB – Registered company number:
6695582

Edited by Andrew Farrow, Adam Miller, and
 Diyan Leake
Designed by Victoria Allen
Picture research by Ruth Blair
Illustrations by Oxford Designers & Illustrators
Originated by Capstone Global Library Ltd
Printed and bound in China by Leo Paper
 Products Ltd

ISBN 978 1 406 23846 4 (hardback)
16 15 14 13 12
10 9 8 7 6 5 4 3 2 1

British Library Cataloguing in Publication Data
Senker, Cath.
Improving healthcare. -- (Charities in action)
362.1'0425-dc23
A full catalogue record for this book is available from
the British Library.

Acknowledgements
The author and publisher are grateful to the
following for permission to reproduce copyright
material: Alamy pp. 35 (© National Geographic Image
Collection), 36 (© Photofusion Picture Library); Corbis
pp. 7 (© Dai Kurokawa/epa), 11 (© Abir Abdullah/
epa), 17 (© STR/epa), 21 (© Hamideddine Bouali/
Demotix), 26 (© Andrew Kent), 28 (© Kristian Buus/
In Pictures), 31 (© Eman Mohammed/Demotix), 48
(© Reuters), 52 (© Kim Kulish); Getty Images pp. 13
(AFP), 22 (Jody Amiet/AFP), 25 (Karen Kasmauski/
Science Faction), 39 (Joos Mind), 42 (Yellow Dog
Productions), 44 (Bloomberg), 55 (Justin Sullivan),
57 (Eco Images); Image courtesy of Jaguar Land
Rover p. 51; photoshot pp. 18 (© EPA), 40 (© Picture
Alliance); Science Photo Library p. 46 (Simon Fraser/
RVI, Newcastle-upon-Tyne).

Cover photograph of an amputee in the Cité Soleil
Médicins Sans Frontières clinic, Port-au-Prince, Haiti,
reproduced with permission of Getty Images
(Alison Wright/National Geographic).

Every effort has been made to contact copyright
holders of material reproduced in this book. Any
omissions will be rectified in subsequent printings if
notice is given to the publisher.

CONTENTS

Words printed in **bold** are explained in the glossary.

WHY DO WE NEED HEALTHCARE CHARITIES?

A wide range of health challenges face our world. In **less economically developed countries (LEDCs)** in particular, governments generally do not have the resources to fund all the health services that are needed. This is why healthcare charities and **non-governmental organizations (NGOs)** become involved.

A charity is an independent organization, not linked to government or business, which is committed to helping people in need. An NGO is another type of association that is not part of government or business and is devoted to a particular cause. There are also **non-profit organizations** that use the money they make to carry out their work, rather than giving the profits to the owners.

Healthcare charities and NGOs not only tackle health problems but also promote genuine health for all. As the World Health Organization (WHO)'s constitution states, "Health is a state of complete physical, mental, and social well-being and not merely the absence of disease or infirmity [long-term weakness]."

Poverty and disease

Many healthcare charities and NGOs focus their efforts on LEDCs: the poorer countries of the world, including the countries of Africa, Asia (except for Japan), South America, and the Caribbean. The greatest healthcare problems arise in LEDCs. The WHO estimates that nearly one-third of disease globally is caused by environmental factors, including malnutrition (lack of sufficient food) and poor water supplies. These conditions overwhelmingly affect people in poverty. Around 10 million children under five years old die each year – at least 30 per cent of them because of severe malnutrition.

War and disaster

Conflict and natural disasters are major creators of health issues. During a war medical facilities are overburdened coping with the injured. They may be destroyed or health workers killed. Transport is affected, making it hard to reach hospitals.

People who escape from the conflict area are often forced to make long journeys on foot, with severe effects on their health. Natural disasters, such as earthquakes, volcanoes, and tsunamis, kill and injure and leave many people homeless and without food or water.

Non-communicable diseases

In both LEDCs and **more economically developed countries (MEDCs)**, **non-communicable diseases (NCDs)** are major killers. These are non-infectious illnesses, such as **cancer**, heart disease, chronic (long-lasting) respiratory diseases, and **diabetes**. NCDs account for about 60 per cent of deaths worldwide. They used to be seen as the diseases of rich countries, but in fact LEDCs are worse affected than MEDCs.

Top ten causes of people worldwide who become sick in a year, in millions

Diarrhoeal disease [b]	4,620.4
Lower respiratory infections [b]	429.2
Malaria [b]	241.3
Serious injuries from accidents or violence	89.7
Complications of pregnancy	50.0
Measles [a]	27.1
Pertussis (whooping cough) [b]	18.4
Malignant neoplasms (tumours)	11.4
Dengue (virus causing flu-like symptoms) [b]	9.0
Stroke, first-ever	9.0
Tuberculosis [a]	7.8
Congestive heart failure	5.7
HIV infection [a]	2.8

Notes

[a] new cases

[b] episodes of disease (people often have an episode of this disease more than once)

Refugees in crisis: a helping hand

September 2010: Community **outreach** nurse Nenna Arnold manages a health post for healthcare charity Médecins Sans Frontières (MSF – "Doctors Without Borders") in Dadaab refugee camp in north-eastern Kenya, Africa. She hears about the newly arrived refugees settling outside the camp. They have fled from violence and **drought** in Somalia.

Nenna goes to assess the situation and is shocked: "It is a group of human beings living in conditions most of us can't imagine. They have no shelter, no plastic sheeting, very little food. Children are even being killed by hyenas because they have no protection."

The Somali refugees have undergone a long, dangerous journey, enduring the threat of wild animals, bandits, and disease as well as hunger and thirst. Few have any belongings. Many of them are ill as well as **malnourished**.

Women and children first

Nenna seeks out the children and pregnant women, taking them to the health post, or the hospital if they are seriously ill. She says, "One young mum was having problems with her pregnancy. She lost the baby, but she lived. Another sick baby was brought to the hospital too late. There was nothing they could do."

Periodically, Nenna visits the new arrivals with a team of community health workers to **vaccinate** the children against life-threatening diseases. They take a loudhailer to call people. "At the latest one, we vaccinated 257 children ... most of whom had never been vaccinated before."

Health posts – a life saver

March 2011: Nenna's team sets up a temporary health post outside the camp because the people here cannot reach the existing ones or do not know what services are available. On the first day they see 165 people and admit 98 malnourished refugees to their nutrition programme.

At times, Nenna says, "I feel overwhelmed by the enormity of it all, but I try to focus on what I can accomplish ... Sundays don't come often enough, and certainly don't last long enough."

However, Nenna goes on to say, "Despite all the difficulties, I really think I have the best job in the whole project ... It's so nice to be able to come out here to the new arrivals' area and to be able to help the people who really need it most."

Assisting Somali refugees, Dadaab

Three vast refugee camps in Dadaab shelter more than 300,000 refugees, mostly from Somalia. One of them is Dagahaley, with over 100,000 inhabitants. MSF runs a 110-bed hospital in Dagahaley, providing paediatric care (medical care for children), maternity, surgical, and nutritional services. It also has four health posts around the camp offering primary healthcare (for people when they first fall ill), vaccinations, care for pregnant women, and mental healthcare. The facilities also serve those living outside the camp's boundaries. The healthcare needs are huge. Many patients suffer respiratory tract infections (to do with the breathing system) or diarrhoea. The hospital deals with an average of 10,000 outpatient appointments per month and around 600 patients are admitted to hospital.

A Somali baby is weighed at a clinic run by MSF in Dagahaley refugee camp, in 2011.

MEDCs: bad habits and poor health

In MEDCs, much of the burden of disease comes from people not looking after their health. Smoking is associated with respiratory illnesses and lung cancer, but it is also a major cause of heart disease. People who regularly drink a lot of alcohol risk a variety of health problems, including cancer, liver damage, and heart attacks. Another serious issue is obesity – being extremely overweight. It increases the risk of heart disease, **stroke**, and cancer and can lead to Type 2 diabetes, a long-term condition caused by having too much glucose in the blood (see page 32).

Although these diseases linked to lifestyle can lead to an early death, improvements in medicine mean that, generally in MEDCs, people are living longer. The proportion of older people in the population is increasing. For example, in both the United States and Australia, nearly one-fifth of the population is over 60. Elderly people tend to have greater healthcare needs than younger people. They may develop eyesight or hearing difficulties or mobility (movement) problems, and can suffer serious injury if they fall.

Mental health

Mental well-being is just as important as physical health. Mental health problems affect around one-quarter of people at some point in their life. The most common are anxiety and **depression**; others include bipolar disorder (severe mood swings), and schizophrenia (having delusions and finding it hard to think straight).

Disability

Fifteen per cent of the world's population have a disability. Disability is a very broad term. It includes people who are unable to walk, such as victims of war who have had a leg amputated (cut off), and those with chronic conditions such as cystic fibrosis (see pages 46–47) or mental illnesses like schizophrenia. Others suffer from blindness or deafness. Some people with disabilities do not have particular health needs; a child born blind may be perfectly healthy otherwise. Yet those with chronic conditions need continual treatment. As a group, people with a disability endure poorer health than the general population.

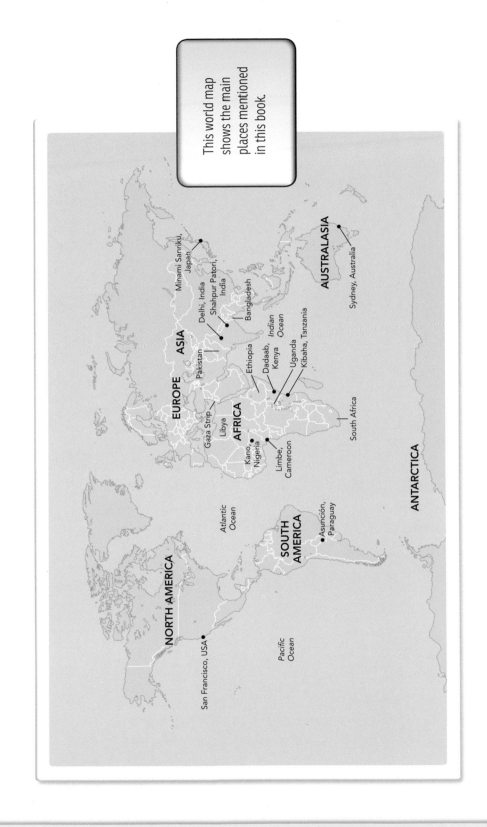

This world map shows the main places mentioned in this book.

NORTH AMERICA

San Francisco, USA

Pacific Ocean

Atlantic Ocean

SOUTH AMERICA

Asunción, Paraguay

ANTARCTICA

EUROPE

ASIA

Pakistan

Minami Sanriku, Japan

Delhi, India

Shahpur Patori, India

Bangladesh

Gaza Strip

Libya

AFRICA

Ethiopia

Dadaab, Kenya

Uganda

Kibaha, Tanzania

Indian Ocean

Kano, Nigeria

Limbe, Cameroon

South Africa

AUSTRALASIA

Sydney, Australia

9

Charities and NGOs have to be well organized so they can respond quickly and effectively in an emergency and plan their long-term work. They need to have clear aims, a plan of action, and to raise funds to pay for their activities.

Strong structures

Large global charities have worldwide, regional, and national structures. The Red Cross has one arm for assisting people in war zones (the International Committee of the Red Cross, ICRC), and another for helping victims of natural disasters (the International Federation of Red Cross and Red Crescent Societies, IFRC). Within countries, it has National Societies, most of which have emergency response teams that can act in their own country and go abroad if needed. The International Conference of the Red Cross and the Red Crescent meets every four years to discuss the organization's plans and coordinate its efforts.

Small charities may have just a handful of people running the whole show. For example, Gilead is a small health development charity in Uganda that delivers health education, supports a clinic, and runs a child sponsorship programme (donors give money towards individual children). Gilead receives overall guidance from the well-respected leader of a large organization. Sponsorship officers organize the sponsorship scheme, while the welfare officers run the clinic and a community hall. A nurse cares for children at the clinic, supervised by a doctor. Another Gilead staff member looks after the piggery, where he teaches local people how to rear healthy pigs. "Gifts for Gilead" is the fundraising arm of the organization.

Sound preparations

As well as having a solid structure, healthcare charities have to be well prepared. In areas prone to natural disaster, they train their staff and local citizens to cope with emergencies. Bangladesh regularly experiences cyclones and floods. The Bangladesh Red Crescent trains community volunteers through the cyclone preparedness programme.

The volunteers learn how to assess the risks caused by cyclones and plan how to react. When Cyclone Sidr hit Bangladesh in November 2007, the volunteers worked all night to **evacuate vulnerable** people, saving thousands of lives. As one volunteer explained, "We call a meeting for all the women, every month. We discuss the signalling system and what action we should take. During Cyclone Sidr, a woman badly injured her leg. We used our first aid training to bandage it with a sari."

Logistics

It is also essential to plan the logistics of an operation – the practical details. In emergencies, healthcare charities coordinate their work with other aid agencies; the ICRC works closely with the WHO, for example. Charities decide between them which group is going to turn up where, and with which supplies. It would be pointless for every charity to bring medical supplies and no one to bring water!

As Cyclone Sidr approached the coast of Bangladesh, these villagers moved towards safe shelters inland. More than 600,000 people had to escape to safety.

Putting plans into practice

Logistics officers take charge of the practicalities. For instance, in October 2010, widespread floods in Pakistan affected 20 million people. Logistics officer Claire Durham was in charge of sending out relief items for the British Red Cross. She described her job at the time: "The British Red Cross logistics team is managing two warehouses – one in Sindh Province and one in Punjab Province ... On a daily basis we're sending out food and other items, like blankets, tarpaulins, and water containers to around 4,200 people."

Long-term projects

All charities plan for the future. Healthcare charities on the frontline, saving lives during crises, plan how to respond more effectively. Health-promotion charities focus on ways to reduce illness – less dramatic but just as important! For example, an NGO called the Canadian Partnership Against Cancer formed a five-year plan for 2008–2012. This included a national cancer prevention initiative to survey environmental hazards that increase the risk of cancer. A strategy was to be developed to address obesity, which also increases the likelihood of cancer. Another element was to develop a scheme to minimize the risk of skin cancer from over-exposure to the Sun.

Operation WellFound is a charity that builds wells and latrines, primarily in Africa. Working in some of the poorest countries in the world, it aims to relieve poverty along with reducing or eradicating disease. The charity brings sustainable solutions to poverty and inequality, resulting in improved independence, dignity, and quality of life. Operation WellFound guarantees that all donations go directly to its projects, with nothing spent on administration or office costs.

Recruitment of staff

Planning, training, and logistics all have to be managed. To run effectively, charities have a management team and a core of paid workers: fundraisers, campaigners, communications officers, and human resources (HR) departments to recruit staff. HR teams seek volunteers to work alongside the employees, using a strict recruitment process. Applicants have to fill in an application form, attend an interview, and provide references – just as if they were applying for a paid job. Charities are extremely professional, and managed in a similar way to businesses.

MSF: recruiting for emergencies

Médecins Sans Frontières is an independent medical aid organization, committed to providing aid where it is most needed. It takes on qualified and experienced health workers and non-medical staff as volunteers. MSF needs financial controllers and logistics officers as well as surgeons, doctors, midwives, and nurses. It is active in conflict zones where many people have been displaced from their homes and medical facilities are poor. Volunteers have to be prepared to work abroad, often in an unstable region of the world. The jobs are tough, demanding, and sometimes dangerous, but they are remarkably rewarding.

So how does MSF have volunteers at the ready so it can respond to emergencies anywhere in the world at any time? Prospective volunteers have to apply online and if they have the right skills and experience, they are invited to an interview. If successful, their names are entered on a register of volunteers. Then the HR Officer tries to match them to a vacancy in the field. It is an extremely competitive process; many people worldwide apply for just a few positions.

Boxes of emergency supplies are gathered in a warehouse in Iwate prefecture, Japan, the region where a massive tsunami hit in March 2011 (see page 17).

The World Health Organization

The World Health Organization (WHO) is an international healthcare NGO for the whole world, with a membership of 193 countries. Its aims are to:

- promote health worldwide;
- defend against outbreaks of disease;
- strengthen health services;
- provide health information;
- encourage partnerships between international, non-profit, and privately run health organizations;
- carry out research into health-related issues.

Shared vision

We have to find a way to work with our different partners ... I think it is important that we have a shared vision."

Dr Margaret Chan, Director-General of WHO from 2007

High-level planning

Each WHO task requires extensive planning. Every year, representatives from the member states and other international health organizations meet at WHO's headquarters in Geneva, Switzerland to plan for the next two years. They also have a medium-term, five-year plan (for example, 2008–2013) and a long-term scheme of work (2006–2015) to wipe out diseases and promote health. In addition, WHO plans how to react to health emergencies caused by pandemics (the rapid spread of serious diseases) and natural disasters such as floods and earthquakes.

The executive board of 34 health experts is responsible for putting the decisions into practice. Work is organized on a regional basis. The member states of WHO are divided into six regions, each with a regional office in charge. From here, experts and workers are sent out to individual countries.

Stop TB: planning at community level

WHO carries out its strategies from the global level right down to local communities. An example is the Stop TB strategy to reduce the numbers of people who die from **tuberculosis (TB)**. (See also page 24.)

To be cured of TB, patients need to take tablets daily for at least six months. Otherwise they may not get better, and a dangerous, **drug-resistant** form of the disease may develop. In most places in the world, patients have to travel to a health centre every day for their medication.

For the people of rural Kibaha in Tanzania, a country with one of the highest rates of TB worldwide, the nearest hospital is too far away. Jane Tibihka, a TB survivor herself, realized that former patients could help out: "They have the understanding and motivation to help others sick with the disease." Jane formed the Upendo Disadvantaged Group. She and 30 other people cured of TB have become community health workers. They look after more than 200 TB patients in the district. The patients pick up their medication monthly and the health workers help them to take it properly. They need to remember to take their tablets every day.

Dr Wawa provides guidance to the health workers: "It is good to advise them [the patients] to take them at the same time of day – for example, when a favourite radio programme is on the air." Upendo's members supply food packages when they can; people need to eat a good diet so they can tolerate the medicines. The group also organizes community gatherings with music and poetry to educate their neighbours about TB.

The Director-General's office oversees the whole WHO charity

Family and community health, e.g. vaccines, childbirth	Health systems and services, such as technology and medicines
General management, e.g. finance and recruiting	**HIV/AIDS**, TB, **malaria** and neglected tropical diseases
Health action in crises, e.g. emergency response	Innovation (new ideas), information, evidence and research
Health security and environment, e.g. food safety and public health policy	Non-communicable diseases and mental health

Healthcare charity workers are often the first on the scene in an emergency. In June 2011, violence broke out in South Kordofan, Sudan, leaving hundreds injured. Volunteers from the Sudanese Red Crescent jumped to the rescue. "They were the first on the ground to serve the affected people, evacuate the injured and wounded, deal with the dead bodies, provide first aid services, and distribute food and non-food items," says their director, Rahama Mohamed Ibrahim. "We are very proud of our volunteers for their dedication."

Rapid response teams

Some charities, such as IFRC, WHO, and MSF, are specifically set up to provide emergency medical aid. Save the Children focuses on supporting children at risk. During a crisis, media images show health workers providing water for endless queues of people, feeding severely malnourished children, and offering materials to build fragile shelters. Yet food, water, and shelter are not the only requirements. A large part of the emergency health response involves preventing malnutrition and illness among those at risk. It includes providing mental health care for those traumatized by frightening events.

Kenya food crisis

During the drought in north-east Kenya in 2009, Save the Children offered emergency medical care and assistance to vulnerable people.

• It used its Children's Emergency Fund to set up 83 remote outreach sites. These provided nutritious food, medicine, and medical treatments to malnourished women and children.

• It provided food vouchers to livestock farmers whose animals had died in the drought so they could buy high-protein foods such as meat and milk.

• It gave cash to the poorest livestock farmers so they would not have to sell their surviving animals.

Japanese earthquake and tsunami

On 11 March 2011, a powerful earthquake measuring 8.9 on the Richter scale hit north-east Japan – the most devastating in its history. It triggered a massive tsunami, with waves up to 10 metres (33 feet) high sweeping away homes, buildings, crops, and vehicles and triggering fires. At least 1,000 people were killed immediately. Thousands of people living near two nuclear power plants had to be evacuated because of the danger of a catastrophic meltdown. The Japanese Disaster Medical Assistance Teams leapt into action, assisted by international healthcare charities.

Aid to survivors

Eric Ouannes, general director of MSF Japan, outlined his organization's response: "Right from the beginning we had a small mobile assessment team moving from one place to another very quickly to cover as much of the devastated area as possible and visit as many evacuation centres as we could."

There were huge challenges in the first few days: "Communication has been very erratic over the past four days ... Transportation is difficult, too. Almost everywhere we have been roads are blocked and there has been a shortage of fuel for our vehicles."

Japanese villagers in Minami Sanriku carry relief supplies, March 2011. Around 390,000 people had to leave their homes and seek refuge in shelters.

Stress and trauma

Within two days, medical needs in evacuation centres grew, so MSF sent four more workers. Two worked with local doctors in the devastated port of Minami Sanriku. Another team of two went to Oshima Island to work in the evacuation centres. The first medical personnel to reach the island, they found around 40 patients who had lost their medication for chronic diseases. The majority were elderly, trying to cope in the freezing temperatures. MSF ordered 25,000 blankets.

A week after the disaster, an MSF psychologist went to assess mental health needs. Ritsuko Nishimae, working with the MSF team, reported: "Many people now are in a phase of acute stress disorder, which is a totally natural response to this level of trauma. If they are not able to get proper support **psychologically**, there is an increased possibility that they could develop **post-traumatic stress disorder**."

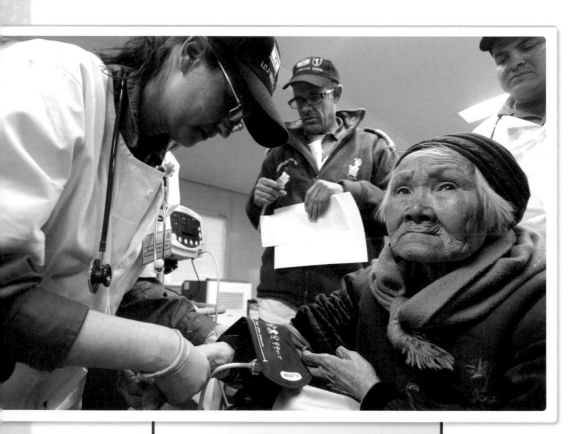

An elderly refugee in Minami Sanriku has her blood pressure checked by a nurse, one of a medical team that came from Israel to assist during the emergency.

The teams continued to work in evacuation centres near the devastated port of Minami Sanriku, looking after elderly patients. They also distributed hygiene kits with soap, toothbrushes, toothpaste, and towels to evacuees. By now, the emergency phase was winding down, and the next phase of work began. In April, MSF set up a café where people could have refreshments and talk informally with mental health staff. It started to rebuild two clinics destroyed by the tsunami.

A Japanese doctor's story

Shintaro Hayashi is a doctor from Sendai in Miyagi, one of the areas worst hit by the earthquake and tsunami. When the earthquake hit, he was working for MSF in Kenya. He managed to contact his wife, who was finding it hard to access food and water, but could not reach some of his friends working in the disaster area. He said, "I couldn't believe what had happened, that my region was so damaged. The people around me in Kenya saw it as an event in another world, but for me it was my problem, my family problem." He decided to return to Japan.

Back in Japan, Hayashi worked in four evacuation centres in the Minami Sanriku area, operating mobile clinics. He aided elderly people with chronic diseases and gave psychological support, which was greatly needed: "Lots of people smile and talk a lot, but I think it's because they are trying their best to survive the situation. The more time passes, if they enter temporary houses on their own, they start to feel depressed or worry about their future." Hayashi noticed how hard people were working in the evacuation sites; relationships in these small communities were strong, and everyone wanted to keep busy and improve their situation: "Work is assigned for different people, and they are always working, constructing a bath, or clearing broken houses. I think it's good for their mental health," he commented, although he believed people needed more psychological support. Hayashi was impressed by the response from within Japan and from international NGOs, but recognized that the disaster would affect the Japanese people for many years to come.

Helping victims of war

Healthcare charities play a vital role in assisting people injured in conflict or displaced from their homes. They set up refugee camps and see to people's medical needs. For example, in February 2011 the international relief and development charity Muslim Aid launched an appeal to provide assistance to Libyans who were enduring escalating violent conflict between rebel forces and those loyal to the government. On the border between Egypt and Libya, Muslim Aid worked with the Egyptian Medical Syndicate to provide emergency medical support for hospitals in Libya.

Muslim Aid also gives ongoing medical and general healthcare support to the country of Iraq, which has experienced conflict since the US-led invasion of 2003. Iraqi health facilities have seriously deteriorated. Muslim Aid has refurbished and equipped clinics and hospitals, and provided them with medicines. It helps **internally displaced persons (IDPs)** with food, clothing, and hygiene kits.

Addressing disability

Injuries during war lead to disabilities for some victims. In LEDCs, resources to help them are scarce, so healthcare charities may step in. Afghanistan, one of the poorest countries in the world, has suffered decades of conflict and remained unstable since the US-led invasion of 2001 toppled the radical Islamic Taliban regime. A survey in 2005 indicated that more than 2.7 per cent of the population suffered from a severe disability – one in five households had a disabled family member.

Many are disabled because of injuries caused by landmines – explosive devices that continue to kill and maim long after a conflict is over. If a person steps on a buried anti-personnel mine, their leg is likely to be ripped off. If it explodes while being handled, it can destroy hands, arms, or the face and chest. Every year, hundreds of Afghanis are injured in these horrific ways. About half of all disabled people are children, around 75 per cent of whom do not attend school. As one disabled man in Kabul, Hazrat Gul, said, "We feel excluded from society. Everything – jobs, education, transport, entertainment – is for the able-bodied ... We're only left on the road to beg and survive."

The international aid organization Handicap International has been working in Afghanistan since the 1980s, educating people about the risks of landmines.

Handicap International also raises public awareness of disability issues and provides **rehabilitation** services such as physiotherapy (exercises to treat injuries), orthopaedic services (treatment for the injuries), and artificial limbs. The charity runs sports activities for disabled people to improve their quality of life and personal development.

Zakah

Most faiths expect their followers to give to charity. For practising Muslims, it is a religious duty to contribute a small proportion of their wealth to charity through a tax called zakah. A range of Muslim charities channel the funds to poor and needy people in their own community and abroad – both Muslims and non-Muslims.

Libyan refugees who have crossed the border into Tunisia arrive at Ras Jedir refugee camp, carrying their possessions.

IMPROVING HEALTHCARE IN LEDCs

As well as responding to emergencies, healthcare charities work to tackle disease and improve health. They provide access to clean water supplies and **sanitation**, treat illnesses, supply medicines, and assist in building hospitals and health centres. Offering mental health support is a high priority, too. Much of their work is in LEDCs, where health problems are worst.

Tackling disease: immunization

A variety of infectious diseases threaten people's lives or cause disability in LEDCs, including polio, measles, yellow fever, hepatitis B, and TB. Immunization is a vital element in controlling and eliminating them. Eight out of ten children in the world are **immunized** against six major childhood diseases.

The immunization campaign is coordinated by the Global Alliance for Vaccines and Immunization (GAVI). It is made up of governments and NGOs, including the Bill and Melinda Gates Foundation, which work together to promote vaccination programmes. These programmes are relatively cheap to implement and they save between two to three million deaths every year. In June 2011, leading drug companies helped GAVI's campaign by announcing a huge drop in vaccine prices for LEDCs. In the same month, donors pledged more than £2.5 billion to support GAVI's work.

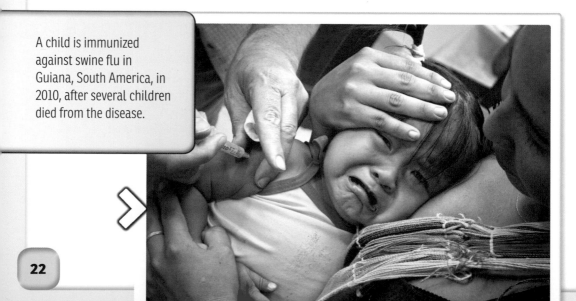

A child is immunized against swine flu in Guiana, South America, in 2010, after several children died from the disease.

Vaccination week

Every year there is a vaccination week, organized regionally. In April 2011, five WHO regions participated at the same time. Health workers, government officials, volunteers, and celebrities took part in special efforts to vaccinate large numbers of people against various diseases.

Estela lives in a village near Assumpción (Asuncion) in Paraguay, South America. She took her three children to the local health centre during vaccination week, where vaccines are offered free of charge. At the centre, the **UNICEF** Regional Director Nils Kastberg addressed the children, "Tell your parents you need vaccines to protect you against disease in the same way that you need a roof over your head to protect you from the rain and Sun." As her baby received polio drops, Estela said, "I am thankful for the health centre because it helps keep my children healthy. They receive vaccines and regular check ups, which is important because there is a lot of sickness among children."

The decade of vaccines

In January 2010, the Bill and Melinda Gates Foundation announced that it would commit £6 billion over the following 10 years for the development and delivery of vaccines to the world's poorest countries. Bill Gates stated: "We must make this the decade of vaccines. Vaccines already save and improve millions of lives in developing countries." He called for donors, governments, and private companies to make efforts to expand vaccination programmes.

The challenge of polio

Estela's baby was immunized against polio; this disease has to be prevented since there is no cure. Polio is highly infectious and affects mainly children under five years old. It invades the nervous system and causes paralysis (loss of control) within hours, usually in the legs. In 1 in 200 cases, the child is paralysed for life and is unable to walk properly.

The Global Polio Eradication Initiative aims to wipe out polio worldwide. A broad alliance led by the WHO, it involves governments, NGOs such as UNICEF, and private companies. Its slogan is "Every last child" – and the aim is to protect all children. This is done through routine immunization of babies and National Immunization Days, organized to catch any children who have missed out.

Stop TB

Another major disease being tackled by healthcare charities is tuberculosis. The Stop TB strategy, launched by WHO in 2006, aims to save 1 million lives by 2015 by preventing and treating TB among people infected with HIV. There is a proven link between TB and HIV: in 2009, nearly 1 in 4 deaths among people with HIV/AIDS were due to TB. If people with HIV who catch TB are treated promptly, many deaths can be avoided.

Tackling tropical diseases

Several tropical diseases, including malaria and river blindness, have devastating effects throughout tropical and sub-tropical countries (near or bordering on the tropics). Malaria is an infectious disease spread by mosquitoes. It can be treated, but the best strategy is to avoid being bitten by mosquitoes. Roll Back Malaria is a global movement that includes the governments of affected countries, private companies, and NGOs. It focuses on providing mosquito bed-nets treated with insecticide, and offering treatment using a drug called artemisinin (see also page 53).

In Nigeria, 1 in 3 children who die young are killed by malaria. Mariam lives in Dawakin Tofa village in Kano, Nigeria. With four children and six grandchildren, she worries constantly about malaria. Up until now, no protection has been available. Through the SuNMap scheme, the Roll Back Malaria partnership is offering long-lasting mosquito nets. Field workers visit every household in Mariam's village and tell them about the nets, handing them a "net card". Mariam takes the card to go to collect nets for her family. There is a long queue and great excitement.

Mariam picks up her nets. Because of the chemicals they contain, she hangs them outside her home to air for 24 hours. The next day, they are ready to use indoors and will give long-term protection against mosquito bites. After providing nets to the inhabitants of Kano province, SuNMap's aim is to extend net provision to every household in Nigeria.

Malaria

- Annual cases: 247 million
- Annual deaths: 881,000; 91% of them in Africa
- Top five countries affected: Nigeria, Democratic Republic of the Congo, Ethiopia, United Republic of Tanzania, Kenya
- Treatment: more than 100 million people
- Nets to prevent malaria: 66.2 million distributed

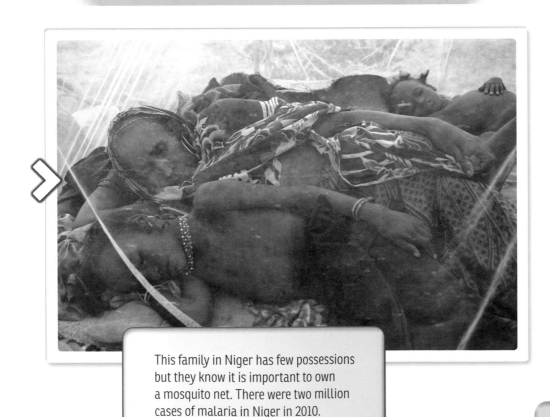

This family in Niger has few possessions but they know it is important to own a mosquito net. There were two million cases of malaria in Niger in 2010.

Sightsavers

The healthcare charity Sightsavers aims to stop preventable blindness in LEDCs by providing specialist treatment and eye care to restore sight. For example, it trains eye surgeons and nurses to remove cataracts, the leading cause of blindness worldwide.

Prevention is always better than cure. Onchocerciasis, or river blindness, is caused by a worm that breeds in fast-flowing rivers in many African countries and some in the Americas. It leads to low vision and blindness. Sightsavers trains community volunteers to distribute the drug Mectizan, which must be taken for 20 years to prevent the disease. The pharmaceutical (drug) company Merck & Co. donates the drug to Sightsavers.

Sightsavers also provides education, counselling, and training to those whose sight cannot be recovered. Health teams visit remote villages to help people who cannot reach health centres easily. They teach blind people daily living skills so they can move around their village, make food, get dressed, and take care of their personal hygiene. Sightsavers trains people to make craft goods or run a small business, or to become rehabilitation workers in their community.

A Thai woman receives a donated pair of glasses from the charity Give the Gift of Sight. Like Sightsavers, it works in LEDCs to restore people's sight.

Free services

The charity offers free eye care to poor people. Dharavi is India's largest slum, made famous by the film *Slumdog Millionaire*. Every day, health workers from the community go from door to door, promoting Sightsavers' free eye-care services. They assist many home workers, who depend on their eyesight for needlework and jewellery making. If they lose their eyesight, they lose their livelihood.

Hirabai's story

Hirabai Bayle is one such person. A 39-year-old woman, she lives with her 14-year-old son, her mother, and four sisters in one tiny room. Hirabai makes a living by stitching gloves at a workshop and selling bananas at the roadside. Five years ago she noticed her eyesight was failing, affecting her work. But she could not afford to have her eyes tested, much less to buy glasses. Fortunately, health worker Jeba Ansari visited Hirabai and tested her eyes. It turned out that Hirabai was long sighted. After an eye screening by a specialist, she received a free pair of glasses.

A day in the life of an ophthalmic nurse

"My name is Goretti Zinkeng and I'm a 42-year-old ophthalmic [eye] nurse in Limbe, Cameroon, in West Africa. I was already a trained nurse when Sightsavers supported me to train in ophthalmology [the study of the eye and its diseases].

"On a typical day, I get up at 5.00 a.m., get dressed, and have breakfast. I attend Catholic mass at 6.00 a.m. and then catch up with my paperwork from 7.30 to 8.00 a.m. From 8.00 a.m. until 2.30 p.m. I'm busy with consultations, giving out glasses and drugs to treat river blindness.

"Sometimes I visit people who have had eye surgery or go out to screen schoolchildren for eye problems. It's part of my job to raise awareness of eye-care services among the public. Often I wear a T-shirt saying 'Take Mectizan' on it. I enjoy my work very much. It's my way of serving God."

Fighting HIV/AIDS

The fatal disease **AIDS** has proved devastating in LEDCs, especially in Sub-Saharan Africa. It is spread through HIV (human immunodeficiency virus), a virus that damages people's **immune system** so they catch diseases easily. AIDS is the final stage of the infection and leads to death.

The strategy for tackling HIV/AIDS is co-ordinated by UNAIDS, an international NGO. It aims to increase access to HIV prevention and treatment that can keep people alive – there is no cure. It has had some success. In 2009, around 1.8 million people died from HIV/AIDS-related diseases, down by one-sixth in five years. However, the rate of HIV infection is rising. There were still two new people infected to every person starting treatment.

Some healthcare charities campaign for the reduction in the cost of AIDS drugs so that more people can be treated. For example, in 2011 a global health partnership, including the Clinton Health Action Initiative, announced that it had achieved a reduction in the price of key drugs for HIV-positive patients. Two drugs would be available at about half the previous price.

These Kenyan children are learning about HIV/AIDS on a laptop provided by Action in the Community Environment. Most of the children have never seen a computer before.

Acting to prevent AIDS

However, AIDS treatment remains costly – and since there is no ultimate cure, HIV prevention work is crucial. Act4Africa is a Christian charity that delivers HIV/AIDS education and promotes changes in behaviour to prevent the spread of AIDS. The charity works with young and vulnerable people in schools, communities, the army, and prison camps, spreading understanding of the disease and encouraging women to protect themselves against HIV infection by using condoms.

Eyewitness: AIDS in Uganda

Helen Miller undertook a medical elective in Jinja, Uganda, with Act4Africa, and witnessed first-hand the heart-breaking tragedy of AIDS:

I am now at the end of my third week in Uganda – I cannot believe how fast the time is flying by ... Having taken a few days to get used to tropical medicine itself, it then took a few more days for me to get my brain around the treatment options, but now I am fully fledged and able to help.

Wednesday was a particularly challenging day – there was only one **intern**, Habbat, plus me, doing the ward round ... When we returned later to check up on patients, I was writing a discharge summary for one child, when one of the mothers from the isolation ward came in and dragged me across the corridor to isolation. When I got there I was met with a heartbreaking sight – an eight-year-old boy, who had been an in-patient for over a month, who was HIV positive and was suffering from TB, had died in his mother's arms ... I knelt down to the mother, put out my hand to her and she clutched it as she cried – my eyes were stinging and I was really struggling to hold it together ... I had taken photographs of the family only two days earlier – they were smiling.

Charities helping children

In 2008, 8.8 million children died before their fifth birthday. Two-thirds of the deaths were from preventable infectious diseases, which could easily be prevented through low-cost treatment and good primary care. Some charities promote better child healthcare. For example, Ben Hewitt, Director of Save the Children's campaign to improve newborn and child survival in Delhi, India, says:

> I was in the Sanjay Colony Cluster in North West Delhi, an hour from the centre of the fastest growing city in the world... People from all over India have moved to Delhi with hopes of a better life but thousands of people are in this cluster with no sanitation or health facilities. The conditions here are shocking... Save the Children is helping by running a life-saving mobile health clinic. The clinic travels to a different location every day including the rubbish tips where the rag pickers rummage through Delhi's leftovers for any scrap to sell. It is an eerie sight, children and adults rummaging through the mountain of rubbish with large black crows circling overhead.

Feel better, live happier

Other healthcare charities specialize in improving people's mental health. Many people in LEDCs are under pressure on a daily basis, worrying about how they are going to make ends meet. Their stress is compounded if they have been involved in violent conflict. They may be affected by trauma for a long time afterwards. Mental health charities focus their efforts on alleviating their troubles.

Muslim Aid supports Nour el Marefa School in Gaza, where many children have been affected by the conflict with Israel. In December 2008, Israel, responding to rocket fire from the Gaza Strip, launched heavy air strikes on the area, and soldiers invaded. Within three weeks, nearly 1,400 Palestinians were killed and tens of thousands of homes were destroyed. Some Nour el Marefa children lost their homes or loved ones. The trauma led many to develop serious behavioural and learning difficulties. Muslim Aid provided funding for additional support for the affected children.

These Palestinians in Gaza attend a school for blind and partially sighted children, funded by the United Nations.

Nour el Marefa school

"Since the war, the children always seem scared. Some have begun to wet themselves, while some have become aggressive. Others are hyperactive or have difficulties in learning; literacy and numeracy problems are common. They find it hard to concentrate or to interact with their peers.

Our school has 20 pupils per class but we take the children to the resources room to receive one-to-one support from a teacher. She uses educational toys to stimulate their brains and make concepts easier to understand. We also arrange psychological therapy sessions for the children and take them on trips. To understand more about their home life and behaviour, we visit the families.

We have noticed an improvement in the children. When they first arrived, they lacked hope but our methods have encouraged them to learn better and feel happier."

Wafr Jabar, English teacher

HEALTHCARE CHARITIES IN MEDCs

Although MEDCs have more resources for health services than LEDCs, healthcare charities still play an important role. They mostly assist people with non-communicable diseases such as cancer and heart disease, disabilities, or mental illness. They help the rising numbers of elderly people and run hospices – homes for individuals who are dying.

The ageing population

Elderly people form a growing proportion of the population in MEDCs, and many of them live alone with no one to care for them. They may have no car and find it hard to use public transport. Healthcare charities such as the Red Cross are on hand to help out. If an elderly person with no support has to attend hospital, a Red Cross transport volunteer takes them there.

For example, Lizzie is a "care in the home" volunteer for the Red Cross. She assists people in her community after they have been discharged from hospital. She explains:

"Generally people suffer from low confidence levels, particularly about being alone and doing things by themselves. Often walking outside can be a bit scary, particularly if they've fallen or collapsed recently, so they can feel quite worried. We give them practical support. We go out and walk with them and help them feel more confident again."

Improving lives

Many charities help people suffering from cancer, heart disease, and diabetes. Diabetes is a serious condition. Some children and young people have Type 1 diabetes: their body does not produce any insulin, the hormone needed to change sugar and starches in food into energy. More common is Type 2 diabetes, in which the body does not produce enough insulin or the cells are unable to use the insulin. People who are overweight have an increased risk of developing Type 2 diabetes. The condition affects a growing number of people in MEDCs – nearly 1 in 10 people in the United States. The American Diabetes Association aims "to prevent and cure diabetes and to improve the lives of all people affected by diabetes". It provides information and diet advice, delivers services to hundreds of communities, and funds research into the prevention and cure of the condition.

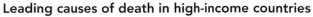

Leading causes of death in high-income countries

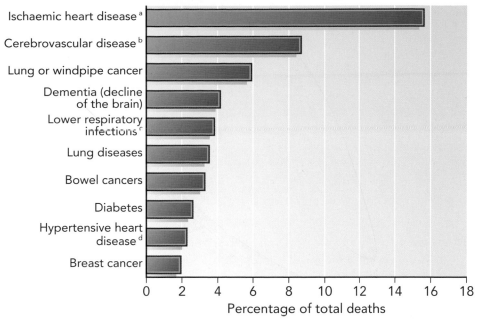

Ischaemic heart disease [a]	
Cerebrovascular disease [b]	
Lung or windpipe cancer	
Dementia (decline of the brain)	
Lower respiratory infections [c]	
Lung diseases	
Bowel cancers	
Diabetes	
Hypertensive heart disease [d]	
Breast cancer	

Percentage of total deaths

[a] Caused by a decreased blood flow because of a narrowing of the arteries
[b] Disease affecting an artery in the brain
[c] Infections such as bronchitis and pneumonia
[d] Heart problems caused by high blood pressure

A dignified end to life

Hospices provide palliative care for people in the final stage of their life – treatment to relieve the symptoms of disease and improve the patient's quality of life. The care may be given in the patient's home, a hospital, or a special hospice building. The staff try to allow patients to live their last days as alert and free of pain as possible, with their loved ones around them.

St Barnabas is a charitable hospice in Worthing, East Sussex, where patients can share their experiences and even enjoy new ones. Rosie had cancer and knew she had only weeks to live. An overseas development worker, dancer, and singer, she always believed she was useless at art. However, an art therapist at St Barnabas helped her to make a short film, *I Can't Draw*, providing a beautiful legacy for her friends and family.

"A support group helped me cope with cancer"

Tylor is from Sydney, Australia. He loved his teenage years. At 17, he had a great group of friends and was really enjoying school. He felt that life didn't get any better than that. "It was as if the gods themselves had a little meeting and said, 'Yeah, look, Ty's life has pretty much reached full enjoyment capacity, so we're gonna take him back down to zero. Let's give him cancer!'"

After Tylor's symptoms appeared, there were trips to the doctor, a variety of tests, and the continual waiting for results. Eventually Tylor was diagnosed with leukaemia (blood cancer). He immediately went into denial that he had cancer. When his mum called his grandparents, he said, "Don't say it's cancer, I've just got a blood disease!" He didn't even tell his friends for nearly two weeks.

Falling into depression

Tylor had to undergo **chemotherapy** at his local hospital and he became depressed for the first time in his life. He woke up late each day, lay in bed for several hours, then just sat in the back yard not doing much at all. It was distressing for his family to see him like this.

CanTeen – support for sufferers

Tylor joined an organization called CanTeen, a support group for young people living with cancer. It allows them to meet others in the same situation and offers trips and activities. But he did not get involved for many months. He felt he was too old for organized activities. Eventually, when he had nearly completed his treatment except for a few **radiotherapy** sessions, he went on his first outing with CanTeen. That day he was feeling quite well.

During the day trip, he met people with whom he formed long-lasting friendships. Meeting others in his situation made the leukaemia easier to cope with, and his only regret was not using the support service earlier, when he was enduring gruelling hospital treatment.

After the cancer treatment, Tylor went back to school for his final year. He still needed "top-ups" of chemotherapy, but only for four days a year. Tylor achieved a place at university and took a year out.

34

He went backpacking in Europe. He says his life has changed since he was diagnosed with cancer: he has different friends, is taking a completely different course from the one he had planned, and has discovered surfing. Owing to the illness, he realizes, "My values and attitudes have shifted, which in turn has affected almost everything else. Priorities in life have reversed."

These children with cancer enjoy an adventurous trip. Child healthcare charities believe that children should not miss out on exciting opportunities just because they are ill.

CanTeen

CanTeen provides support for young people with cancer by:

- offering a peer network across the country for 12- to 24-year-olds and their families
- providing an online community for discussion
- providing a range of free information resources
- offering a counselling service for young people with cancer, or who have been bereaved
- organizing day trips and camps with recreational activities.

Halting harmful behaviour

Some charities address damaging life choices and encourage people to reduce their smoking and drinking. For instance, the Quit Group in New Zealand helps people to stop smoking. Smokers can access support online, by telephone or by text, and the charity provides cheap nicotine patches, gum, and lozenges to help them to overcome the chemical addiction. The charity provides a forum for discussion – bloggers share their experiences on the Quitline website. One young woman explained how Quitline helped her to stop smoking: "The blogs made me feel like I had someone to talk to about quitting. Blogging gave me a chance to get whatever I was feeling off my chest and I didn't use any patches or gum."

Healthier lifestyles

Other charities focus on improving health in the community. They provide information to promote positive habits, such as adopting a good diet. It is estimated that up to 40 per cent of Australian children regularly miss breakfast, which many nutritionists believe is the most important meal of the day. This figure is higher among poor students.

Children in the north of England come to a breakfast club to have a healthy breakfast before school. The Red Cross runs the club.

In Australia, the Good Start Breakfast Club run by the Red Cross offers a healthy breakfast to schoolchildren in deprived areas. The Red Cross finds sponsors to fund the scheme, and volunteers prepare and serve the food.

Promoting mental health

A variety of mental health charities raise awareness of conditions such as depression and schizophrenia, and offer support to sufferers and their families. The South African Depression and Anxiety Group (SADAG) helps people with these common problems. It provides information on its website, runs awareness days and schemes in schools, and has a rural outreach programme. SADAG has a crisis helpline too. In schools, it runs a suicide prevention week. There is a link between serious depression and suicide.

As Zane Wilson, SADAG's founder says:

> We get calls ranging from a teen girl of 15 who has been constantly abused by her stepfather, a boy who has lost his elder brother due to gang violence, and a child of 12 whose mother has recently died of AIDS; sometimes they feel there is nothing to look forward to or that life would be less painful if they were to end it.

SADAG counsellors explain that depression is treatable and that the young people can recover.

Ron Artest: "You don't have to be afraid"

Ron Artest, the well-known basketball player for the Los Angeles Lakers, supports mental health charities, and counselling programmes within schools in particular. He tries to reduce the stigma (shame) attached to mental illness. In June 2010, he spoke out to young people about growing up in a family with a history of mental illness and urged them to speak to school counsellors about their problems: "That doesn't mean you're crazy, it just means you have some issues in your life. This is a way to be able to talk to somebody about your problems."

When disaster hits somewhere in the world, healthcare charities and NGOs rush out urgent appeals to their members and to the public for donations to fund emergency care. Yet they need money on an ongoing basis, not just in a crisis. How do they keep up the momentum?

In times of crisis, healthcare charities often work together to raise funds to help the victims. In the United Kingdom, for example, the Disasters Emergency Committee (DEC) is an **umbrella organization** for 14 agencies that focus on healthcare. The DEC relies on the media and also the banks, post office, and many companies to raise awareness of disasters and encourage donations.

Coping with compassion fatigue

Unfortunately, once disasters are no longer in the news, the general public tend to lose interest quickly. There are so many charities asking for support that it is hard for many people in times of economic crisis to respond to all the requests for donations. They experience **compassion fatigue**. Yet charities constantly need to raise money, so they adopt different strategies.

For example, The International Federation of Red Cross and Red Crescent Societies (IFRC) raises funds continuously at all levels, from international appeals down to the local branches. It also holds a special fundraising week. In the eastern European country of Georgia in 2011, the Georgia Red Cross Society raised funds to support children who had been affected by the armed conflict in 2008. Donation boxes were placed in schools in the capital Tbilisi. Volunteers also collected money on the streets, and the society held a folk-music fundraising event.

Charity shops

Some healthcare charities run charity shops to raise funds. The shops are usually run by paid staff, alongside a team of volunteers. Linda works at an American Cancer Society Discovery Shop in California, USA. The shop sells high-quality donated goods, including clothing, accessories, jewellery, furniture, and artwork. She says, "I volunteer at the Discovery Shop because it keeps me connected with my community. It also gives me the opportunity to work with proactive people [individuals who make things happen] in trying to find the cure for cancer. I know I make a difference."

Many customers appreciate the shops. One visitor to a California Discovery Shop commented, "The best of both worlds – the give and take, in support of each other. This is a hugely beautiful idea – designer clothes, affordable, gently used, and the shop run by warm, open, genuinely caring individuals."

A woman tries on a pair of boots in a charity shop. Charity shops often offer good-quality items at prices far lower than in the regular shops.

The fundraising professionals

Fundraising is a professional business that involves a variety of skills:

- Copy writers produce lively publicity materials about a charity project to encourage businesses and individuals to donate money.
- Public relations (PR) experts work hard to get stories about a charity's work into newspapers, magazines, radio, and TV.
- Advertising teams promote services or products for sale that a charity produces.
- Marketing professionals spread the message through the media and directly to the public.
- Event managers organize and manage a charity's fundraising events.

Celebrity connections

Well-known charities frequently ask celebrities to help them to raise awareness of their work. The more people know about the charity, the more likely they are to donate! WHO invites famous people from the world of art, literature, sport, or entertainment to become "goodwill ambassadors" and assist in spreading a health message.

Top Ethiopian supermodel Liya Kebede became a goodwill ambassador for Maternal, Newborn, and Child Health in 2005. She set up her own charity, the Liya Kebede Foundation, to work with WHO to channel funds to health programmes for mothers and new babies. Her work has been widely publicized in the media, and she has participated in WHO events. In 2006, she spoke about the shocking lack of health services in her own country:

> As a native of Ethiopia, I was familiar with the terrain, but rarely had the opportunity to visit rural health centres, where hospital rooms are barren, lacking basic essential birthing equipment, and there are only a handful of overworked and underpaid medical staff tending to dozens of desperate patients.

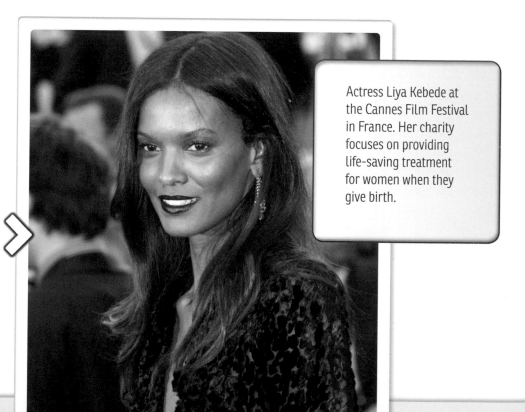

Actress Liya Kebede at the Cannes Film Festival in France. Her charity focuses on providing life-saving treatment for women when they give birth.

As well as raising awareness, some celebrities organize fundraising activities. After the devastating Japanese earthquake and tsunami in March 2011, the singer Lady Gaga raised funds to aid the victims, and contributed a song to a charity album. In June, she performed at a special celebrity charity event, MTV's Video Music Aid Japan, for the Japanese Red Cross. Hosted by the popular Japanese girl band AKB48, the concert featured international and Japanese artists and was designed to inspire young people to contribute money or time to the Red Cross's recovery efforts.

Small charities, thinking local

Big charities with plenty of resources can finance high-profile campaigns to persuade people to donate. But how do small charities raise funds? They try to build strong relationships with their local supporters by attending fundraising events and encouraging donors to become involved with their work. A small charity will create links with the local media and provide interesting stories so that they will report on the charity's work.

Fundraising ideas

Charities ask their supporters to fundraise for them. Here are some activities that often prove successful:

- Coffee mornings, breakfasts, or dinners
- Parties
- Concerts and gigs
- Movie or karaoke nights
- Car-wash service
- Bake sales
- Charity auctions
- Sponsored activities, such as sports events

Eva Longoria

Eva Longoria is best known for starring in the mega-hit series *Desperate Housewives*. Off-screen, she plays an important role in charitable ventures, including healthcare charities. She is the national spokesperson for Padres Contra El Cancer (Parents Against Cancer), a US NGO that works to improve the quality of life for Latino children (of Latin-American origin) with cancer. It provides their families with educational, financial, and language resources.

Zachary, fundraiser for CHOCS

Children Helping Other Children Smile (CHOCS) is an international school fundraising project. The students raise money for children's charities around the world that assist young people living in poverty or suffering from health conditions or disability. For example, the Masorti Bar/Bat Mitzvah Project in Israel helps disabled young people to do their bar or bat mitzvah, an important Jewish rite of passage. Shika in Tanzania assists children who have lost their parents to HIV/AIDS. They often live in poverty with their extended families, housed in mud huts without water or electricity, and are at risk of malaria.

Zachary Narvaez, aged 14, has organized many fundraising events for CHOCS. He recommends running stalls that sell cakes, homemade goods such as bookmarks, or second-hand games and books. Other options include putting on a show, quiz, or other event where people pay an admission charge. But it is best to keep it simple! For Zachary, fundraising is "like running a mini business, and I find organizing and running things great fun and very exciting".

Asking people to sponsor you to run a race is a great way to raise money for a charity.

Getting organized

First, Zachary decides what to do and then gathers a team of friends together. They discuss how to run the event and who will take on which role. Then he finds a location and checks the arrangements with the owner. Next he makes posters and leaflets with the details of the event and the cause, sometimes including a map of the venue. He puts them in as many places as possible. His team makes products to sell at the event.

Zachary finds that holding a raffle raises lots of money if you have good prizes. He contacts local shops, both large and small, to ask them to provide raffle prizes. He says, "I don't email as I find they all say I should call head office or take a letter to the store manager. Get a letter, saying about the charity, the event, and the details and what you want; make sure it has the charity number on and your contact details on it so it looks official." Young people should check with their parent or carer about how the store should contact them – they might prefer the communications to go through them.

A good feeling

Then the big day arrives! Zachary says, "I make sure I am organized and make the area look nice and put posters up to bring people in and sell everything I can. I give stickers to people who donate or buy something." After the event "you get the best feeling knowing how much you helped".

How to organize a fundraising event
- Decide on the event
- Plan: date and time; location; resources; helpers
- Publicity: leaflets; contact the media; advertise in media and social media
- Look for local businesses or sponsors to finance it or supply prizes
- Make plans for the event itself
- Thank everyone involved.

The root cause of many health problems in the world is poverty. Most people who die before their time have fallen prey to diseases that are easily curable by simple methods. Yet scientific and technological breakthroughs can also make a dramatic difference to health outcomes. Many healthcare charities raise substantial funds for research and development.

Scientific research

New diseases continually appear, such as HIV/AIDS in the 1980s, while older diseases mutate. For example, each year the flu virus changes. Scientists are continually racing to find cures for these new conditions. The search for a method to prevent HIV infection continues unabated, with various developments along the way. In 2010, the non-profit Centre for the Aids Programme of Research in South Africa trialled a vaginal gel to protect women whose partners refuse to use a condom. In the trial, the gel reduced the number of women infected by HIV by 39 per cent after two-and-a-half years. According to researcher Dr Salim Abdool Karim, the gel is a cheap product that costs "just pennies".

A scientist analyses a sample from a patient at Gilead Sciences, a US company that is starting to produce cancer medicines.

The battle against cancer

Another disease that has proved extraordinarily difficult to cure is cancer. In the United States, for example, brain cancer affects more than 200,000 people every year. It occurs when cells multiply in an abnormal way in the brain, causing a tumour. Tumours are graded 1 to 4; grade 3 or 4 tumours are malignant, or cancerous. They grow quickly and can spread to other parts of the brain or spine. Surgeons can remove the tumour, but high-grade tumours often return and kill the patient.

US cancer charities have spearheaded trials for a brain cancer vaccine. Vaccines are a new approach to fighting cancer, developed over the last decade. The concept is the same as for a vaccine against a disease like measles. An injection prompts the body's immune system to fight the cancer. The vaccine is tailored to the individual's own tumour and is less toxic than the usual treatments, such as chemotherapy and radiotherapy. The trials are still going on but results so far are encouraging.

Miles for Hope

Bob Gibbs set up Miles for Hope with his wife Barb after he survived brain cancer. The charity's mission is to raise awareness of brain cancer, and also raise funding for new vaccines and treatments. The money comes from members participating in sponsored athletic events.

Bob had a grade 4 tumour. He took the experimental vaccine DCVax. Usually this vaccine raises the average survival rate of patients with grade 4 tumours from 14.6 months to over three years. By 2011, Bob had defied the odds by surviving for seven years. He became determined to promote brain-cancer vaccines. In July 2011, Miles for Hope announced it had formed a partnership with two NGOs to award a research grant to the University of California in Los Angeles, USA, to begin a **clinical trial** for a vaccine for people with low-grade brain tumours.

Cystic fibrosis: waiting for a cure

Cystic fibrosis (CF) is a life-threatening inherited disease. It affects the internal organs, particularly the lungs and digestive system, by clogging them with thick, sticky mucus. This makes it difficult to breathe and to digest food. Only half of sufferers are likely to live past their late thirties.

Scientists have identified the gene that causes CF and hope that they will be able to replace the faulty gene with a normal one. Researchers from the UK CF Gene Therapy Consortium have developed a gene therapy product that is made from a healthy copy of the gene, and a carrier to get it to the right place in the lungs. It is hard to administer gene therapy to the lungs because they have evolved to keep out unknown particles. However, scientists believe they can overcome the difficulties. They have managed to deliver a single dose of gene therapy to volunteers.

One dose will not make a patient better, so the next step is a multi-dose trial. This involves giving volunteers a dose every month for a year. By the end of the trial, the researchers will know if gene therapy helps patients' medical condition to improve. If it is successful, the treatment could be made available a few years later.

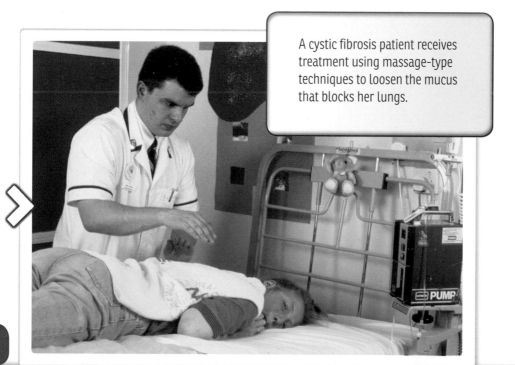

A cystic fibrosis patient receives treatment using massage-type techniques to loosen the mucus that blocks her lungs.

Sophie's race against time

Sophie is a young woman with CF. Her hopes for a healthy future rest with the successful outcome of the gene-therapy trials. Currently, she does everything she can to keep herself healthy: "Every day I go running to help to clear the mucus and stop it from sticking in my lungs. I do as much as I can to keep my lungs in the best condition so I'll benefit if a treatment is found. Once the damage is done, it can't be corrected. My lungs must be as healthy as possible."

Sophie is racing against time. She knows that many people with CF end up in a wheelchair, breathing oxygen from cylinders 24 hours a day. "I hope that gene therapy becomes a reality within a few years before my condition worsens. Otherwise, there will come a point when there's nothing anyone can do. It's scary to think about the future." Yet for Sophie, knowing that a cure is possible motivates her to keep fit.

At the mercy of donors

The UK CF Gene Therapy Consortium planned to start the multi-dose trial in mid-2011. They had manufactured the drugs, and 200 volunteers were ready to take part. However, in June 2011, the Consortium hit a non-scientific barrier. Owing to the economic crisis, donations by the public had fallen, and the funding ran out. Having spent £30 million so far, the consortium was now short of £6 million. As Professor Eric Alton, the consortium's coordinator, explained, "We have had to suspend operations because our money has run out. We are already laying off staff. It is horrendous."

Investing in new technology

Healthcare charities promote new technologies as well as scientific breakthroughs. For example, technological developments in orthopaedics (the branch of medicine concerned with injuries of the bones and muscles) are vital in the treatment of landmine victims, who often have to have a limb amputated. The problem overwhelmingly affects LEDCs that have endured conflict and which generally do not have adequate medical services to support disabled people.

The ICRC and other charities provide orthopaedic devices, including artificial limbs, wheelchairs, and walking aids. The ICRC has developed the polypropylene prosthetic (artificial limb) system. This technology is cheaper than the earlier systems and is now widely used by most organizations assisting landmine victims.

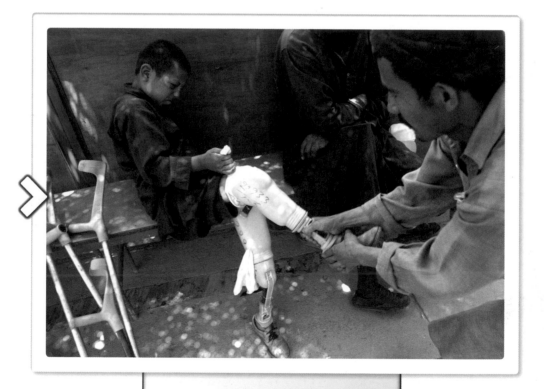

This eleven-year-old boy lost both of his legs in a landmine blast. Another landmine victim helps him to take off his tightly fitting artificial legs.

A new leg twice a year

Tesfahun Hailu from Ethiopia knows what it is like to experience losing a limb. At 13 years old, he lost his leg when a landmine exploded. Tesfahun lived in a small village and had to travel a long way for hospital treatment. Fortunately, once he had recovered from the terrible accident, the ISRC Special Fund for the Disabled provided him with an artificial leg and he was able to return to school. He says, "I was so eager to walk. When the limb-fitting centre gave me my first artificial leg, I started running and the thing broke!"

He later learnt about the Prosthetic Orthotic Centre in the capital Addis Ababa, which manufactures lighter legs, making it easier to walk. Tesfahun has had to have a new leg every six months because he has grown so quickly. Now he is 19 and has finally stopped growing! With the assistance of technology provided by ISRC, and his own determination, Tesfahun has plans. "Even with a disability, you can do almost everything, but it does take hard work. Me, I plan to go to university to study to become a doctor. In the village where I live, there is only one doctor for 6,000 people. We need more doctors."

Hope for Children

Small charities, such as Hope for Children in Sri Lanka, also help landmine victims. A project based in the capital, Colombo, sends out a mobile unit to rural and remote areas to provide prosthetic limbs for disabled children and young adults who lost limbs in landmine accidents. Each child is measured up for a replacement limb, which is made in a workshop. It costs just £100 to provide a limb and a fresh start for a disabled child.

Getting the message out

Healthcare charities increasingly use the latest information and communications technology to deliver health information and services. For instance, on the Australian Diabetes Council website users can find out about diabetes and watch videos on the "Diabetes Channel" in which individuals of all ages and backgrounds explain how they manage their condition.

With persistent healthcare problems in the world, the challenges to governments and healthcare charities remain vast. Charities and NGOs are planning for the future by teaming up with private companies and seeking innovative ways to develop cheap, safe treatments. Out in the field, they train people to deliver healthcare in their own communities.

Partners in the private sector

In recent years, many NGOs and charities have started to work in partnership with private companies – for example, to research medical treatments.

Some argue that there are disadvantages to private businesses undertaking research. The companies compete with each other to make a breakthrough, which is wasteful of resources. For instance, many different organizations are devoted to finding a cure for breast cancer. Wouldn't it be better to have one publicly funded organization?

Others contend that in difficult economic times, it is hard for charities to raise funds – and governments do not offer sufficient public money for medical research. Private drug companies provide an alternative source of funding and can help to discover affordable treatments. It benefits the drug companies, too. If they develop a successful drug, they will make profits, even if they keep the price relatively low.

Additionally, many businesses like to demonstrate corporate social responsibility – to show that they care about social problems. It is good for their image to be seen assisting a healthcare charity. For example, the vehicle production company Land Rover helps the Red Cross in emergencies (see panel opposite).

Local people, local solutions

Another trend in healthcare charity work is the training of local health workers to deliver services in their own community. They support the work of doctors and nurses by offering health education, referring sick people to a clinic, or delivering medicines to people's homes.

Jaime Fernando Aime is employed by MSF to persuade the people of Lichinga in northern Mozambique to be tested for HIV so that those who have the virus can receive life-saving treatment. He stands up in the Accident and Emergency room in Lichinga's hospital and tells everyone he is HIV positive and has been taking **antiretroviral treatment** for four years. He shows the audience his pills, saying "Look, there's nothing to it, it's just medicine, and it means I can live and work normally ... I even cycled here today!"

Emergency vehicles

In 2010, Land Rover made a commitment to the IFRC to provide vehicles so that aid workers could reach vulnerable people quickly after a disaster. During the catastrophic floods in Pakistan in 2010, many roads and bridges were badly damaged. Land Rover donated 110 vehicles, like the one shown here, to the Pakistan Red Crescent Society. They are designed to travel through rough terrain and enabled IFRC workers to deliver much-needed food, clean water, shelter, and medical supplies to thousands of people in the worst affected, remote communities.

OneWorld Health

OneWorld Health (OWH) is the first non-profit drug development organization. Founded and run by Victoria Hale in San Francisco, USA, its mission is "to discover, develop, and deliver safe, effective, and affordable new treatments ... for neglected infectious diseases afflicting children and other vulnerable populations in LEDCs."

How does OWH do this? It works with large pharmaceutical companies to research the possibilities for new drugs. OWH partners with companies to produce synthetic (non-natural) drugs. Then it fast tracks the testing of the drugs in clinical trials to ensure they are safe. Safety tests completed, the organization works with drug manufacturers in the country where the medicines are needed. OWH trains local healthcare workers to bring the treatment to the people who need it most.

Treating kala azar, saving lives

OWH has discovered, designed, and delivered an injection to treat kala azar. This disease, caused by sandfly bites, causes high fever, dramatic weight loss, swelling of the liver and spleen, and anaemia. If untreated, it can kill the victim.

The founder of OneWorld Health, Victoria Hale, with her Chief Medical Officer. OWH develops treatments for diseases that were neglected because other companies believed they could not make money from them.

Bawli Devi's son almost died from kala azar. She lives with her husband Harendra, mother-in-law, and their seven children in a small village near Patori in Bihar, India. They make just £35 per month from selling clothes. Bawli was in despair when her four-year-old son Shivam became gravely ill. He had developed kala azar at the age of two. Now aged four, he was extraordinarily thin and weak, and suffered from a fever. The family borrowed money from relatives to take Shivam to the local rural medical practitioner. "He gave injections and pills to no avail," says Bawli. "We were referred ... to Dr A. K. Thakur, a trained medical doctor at the iOWH [Institute for OneWorld Health] clinic."

Dr Thakur suspected that Shivam had kala azar. Left untreated, the boy would almost certainly die. There was no time to waste. Dr Thakur conducted tests in the laboratory and began a 21-day course of treatment, using a new cheap, safe therapy developed by OWH called Paromomycin IM Injection. The family commuted daily from their village to the clinic, mostly walking. Bawli says, "We braved rain, flood, and strong wind during all 21 days of treatment."

OWH's innovative drugs

- OWH is working on a synthetic drug to provide fast relief from the symptoms of diarrhoea to be used alongside the current treatment, oral rehydration therapy.

- In Africa, OWH is helping to provide treatment for malaria. One of the vital drugs, artemisinin, is in short supply. OWH is producing a synthetic version at an affordable price.

- In Vietnam and India, OWH is working on a treatment for hookworms. These are parasites in the intestines that can affect children's physical and mental development.

HOW YOU CAN GET INVOLVED

How could you support healthcare charities? Most are run by paid staff, but rely on support from volunteers. You could become a volunteer yourself, help people in your community, or raise funds for a worthwhile cause. Plenty of opportunities exist for young people.

Why volunteer?

If you volunteer with a healthcare charity, you will gain valuable experience and important skills. Volunteering enables you to make friends with people outside your normal social circle and helps you to feel part of your local community. You will learn to get on with different kinds of people. Later, you can include voluntary work on your **CV**, which will be useful for future college and job applications. Employers always look for "people skills" in potential employees.

Help local people

You may be able to offer your services close to home. Perhaps you have a neighbour who has just come out of hospital and would like some shopping delivered. Maybe you know someone who is partially sighted and would like some help with reading their post or the newspaper. Always discuss your ideas for volunteering with a parent or carer to ensure that you stay safe while helping out.

Learn to save a life

You never know when an emergency could arise, so learning basic first-aid skills is extremely worthwhile. Some healthcare charities offer courses. Since many young people help to care for younger siblings and other children, the American Red Cross runs a Red Cross Babysitting course to teach them to protect children from danger.

Eleven-year-old Estee Dechtman took the course. One evening, she was playing with her two younger brothers and a friend who has asthma. At some point, her two-year-old brother Isaac opened the friend's bag. When the friend went to take his medication a little later, it had disappeared. After looking around, the anxious children asked Isaac if he had eaten it – and he said yes.

Estee knew exactly what to do. She told her dad what had happened, and was able to give him the local poison-control phone number that she had learned on her course. They called the number – and fortunately it turned out that Isaac had not eaten enough of the drug to cause him harm. But Estee had proved just how useful first aid training can be.

Where can you volunteer?

- Duke of Edinburgh's Award scheme (ages 14–25): You undertake a volunteer placement as well as developing a new skill, doing a physical activity, and going on an expedition.
- St John Ambulance Cadets (ages 10–17): You learn first aid skills, volunteer in your local community, and develop important life skills.
- The Scout Association (ages 6–25): Scouts undertake a variety of outdoor, adventure, and community activities.

As part of your research, ensure you find voluntary work that is suitable for your age group.

Educate your peers

Peer education is another option. Peer educators train to help the people around them to adopt healthier behaviour. The New Jersey Teen Prevention Education Program (Teen PEP) is a peer education initiative in New Jersey, USA, that motivates high-school students to make sensible decisions about their health.

The students on the programme receive information about sexual health. They learn how to educate others to help them to avoid unwanted pregnancy, HIV, and other sexually transmitted infections (STIs). They also advise on how young people can protect themselves from sexual harassment and "date rape" (being forced by someone they know to have sex). Those who participate in the programme become more likely to communicate about sexual health issues with family, friends, and partners, and to use birth-control methods if they are sexually active. It is a positive experience for the volunteers. As one peer educator commented, "It has brought me to a new level of self worth and confidence. I'm not only helping people I don't even know, but I'm helping myself in every other relationship I will ever have."

Raise money

You might prefer to fundraise for a healthcare charity. Do you know someone with a disability or long-term illness? You could support a charity that helps them by organizing a special event (see pages 42–43). Alternatively, you could volunteer in a charity shop to help raise funds.

Kids for World Health

Some young people even set up their own charity! Kids for World Health (KFWH) was founded by third-grade (Year 4) schoolchildren in 2001–2003 in Larchmont, New York City, USA after they saw a TV programme about sleeping sickness. The children learnt that in Africa, large numbers die from this horrific disease that causes swelling of the brain and great sleepiness, eventually leading to a coma (deep unconscious state). A cure existed but was often not available in the poor communities where it was desperately needed.

The children formed KFWH as a non-profit organization and linked up with WHO and MSF. Other schools formed branches of KFWH and joined the campaign. They raised funds that were used to build the first KFWH clinic in Yei, Sudan.

Since then, they have set up other clinics in Duk County in Sudan, Kaliua in Tanzania, and Otoboi Sub-county in Uganda. All together, their clinics provide more than half a million local villagers with treatment for sleeping sickness and other little-known tropical diseases. Through KFWH, the children have put into practice their belief that "Life is important for all people of the world, rich or poor."

Health workers in the Ivory Coast, West Africa, test villagers' blood to see if they contain the parasites (tiny animals that live in another animal or human) that cause sleeping sickness.

How to find out more

• Your local library will have information about healthcare charities that are seeking help.

• Look in the phone directory to find which healthcare charities have a branch in your area.

• Contact your local volunteer bureau to discover current opportunities.

• Volunteer bureaux have websites where they advertise volunteering vacancies.

Note: Always check the minimum age for volunteering jobs.

FACTS AND FIGURES

In 2000, world leaders adopted the Millennium Development Goals, which aimed to reduce world poverty and improve global healthcare by 2015. Here are some of the achievements in healthcare brought about by governments, NGOs, and healthcare charities.

Global burden of disease	Improving healthcare
Around 10 million children under the age of five die each year.	Child deaths fell from 12.4 million in 1990 to 8.1 million in 2009.
Malnutrition is the underlying cause of at least 30% of deaths of children under five.	The percentage of underweight children under five years old is estimated to have dropped from 25% in 1990 to 16% in 2010.
Cardiovascular diseases (of the heart and blood vessels) are the number-one cause of death in the world.	At least 80% of these deaths could be prevented through a healthy diet, regular physical activity, and avoiding smoking; healthcare charities are working to promote these.
HIV/AIDS is still the leading infectious killer in the world, and is the leading cause of adult death in Africa.	Deaths from AIDS peaked in 2004, when 2.2 million people died. The number dropped to 1.8 million in 2009.
For every two individuals who begin treatment for HIV each year, five people are newly infected with HIV.	• New HIV infections declined by 17% from 2001 to 2009. • From 2003 to 2008, the number of people receiving antiretroviral therapy for HIV increased by ten times, from 400,000 to 4 million, or 42% of the people who needed treatment.
Tuberculosis is the second leading infectious killer.	The number of tuberculosis cases in LEDCs fell from 310 per 100,000 of population in 1990 to 210 in 2008.

Global burden of disease	Improving healthcare
In 2008, malaria caused nearly one million deaths, mostly among African children.	Worldwide production of mosquito nets to protect against malaria increased five times from 2004–09, from 30 million to 150 million nets.
More than 350,000 women die every year owing to preventable complications during pregnancy or childbirth. Nearly all the deaths (99%) occurred in LEDCs.	• The number of women dying from complications during pregnancy and childbirth decreased by 34% between 1990 and 2008. • The proportion of women who received skilled assistance during childbirth rose from 53% in 1990 to 63% in 2008.
In LEDCs, 1–5% of children with measles die from complications of the disease.	Routine immunization against measles rose from 70% of children in LEDCs in 2000 to 81% in 2008.
Around 15% of the world's population have some form of disability. Hearing loss, vision problems, and mental disorders are the most common causes of disability.	Community-based rehabilitation (CBR) is being implemented in 90 countries to address the needs of people with disabilities.

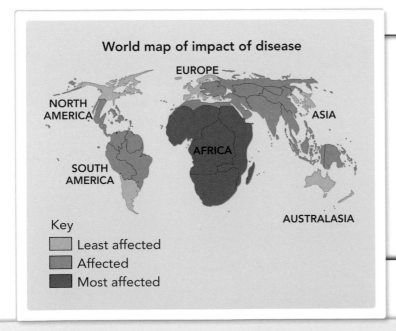

World map of impact of disease

EUROPE

NORTH AMERICA

ASIA

AFRICA

SOUTH AMERICA

AUSTRALASIA

Key
- Least affected
- Affected
- Most affected

This map has been resized to show the burden of disease. For example, Africa is shown large because it has a high burden of disease, while North America is tiny because its burden is low.

GLOSSARY

AIDS *see* HIV/AIDS

antiretroviral treatment treatment that suppresses or stops HIV, which is a kind of virus called a retrovirus

cancer serious disease in which cancer cells form in the body and kill normal body cells

chemotherapy treatment for cancer with the use of chemical substances

clinical trial testing a new drug on patients to see if it is safe and effective

compassion fatigue gradual lessening of compassion over time; for example, when there are so many stories of suffering in the media that people grow tired of them and become less likely to offer money to charities to help out

CV stands for the Latin words *curriculum vitae*, meaning an account of the things you have done in your life

depression medical condition that makes a person feel very sad and anxious

diabetes medical condition that means the body cannot produce and use insulin, the hormone needed to change sugar and starches in food into energy

drought long period of time when there is little or no rain

drug-resistant when bacteria or viruses that cause disease adapt so that drugs that used to kill them no longer do so

evacuate move from a place of danger to a safer place

HIV/AIDS the HIV virus damages the immune system so that the sufferer catches diseases easily. If no treatment is given, HIV infection causes AIDS, which leads to death.

immune system the system in your body that produces substances that help it to fight against infection

immunize protect a person from disease, usually by giving them an injection of a vaccine

intern person who works to gain practical experience in a job, usually as a volunteer

internally displaced person (IDP) person who has been forced to leave home and move to a different part of the country

less economically developed country (LEDC) one of the poorer countries of the world, including those in Africa, Asia (except for Japan), South America, and the Caribbean

malaria disease caused by the bite of some mosquitoes, which can be fatal

malnourished not having enough to eat or enough of the right kinds of foods

more economically developed country (MEDC) one of the richer countries of the world, including those in Europe, North America, and Australia

non-communicable disease (NCD) disease that cannot be caught from another person

non-governmental organization (NGO) organization that is not part of government or business and does not make a profit

non-profit organization organization that uses the money it makes to further its own goals rather than distributing it to owners or shareholders

outreach organization that provides a service to people where they live so they do not have to travel to a hospital or clinic

post-traumatic stress disorder medical condition in which a person suffers mental and emotional problems resulting from a deeply shocking experience

psychological connected with a person's mind; a psychologist is a person trained in psychology who treats people with mental disorders

radiotherapy the treatment of disease (usually cancer) by using radiation

rehabilitation helping people to have a normal life again after they have been very ill

sanitation the equipment and systems that keep places clean, especially by removing human waste

stroke sudden serious illness caused by a burst or blocked blood vessel in the brain

tuberculosis (TB) serious infectious disease in which swellings appear on the lungs and other parts of the body

umbrella organization an organization that coordinates several organizations working together

UNICEF an agency of the United Nations established in 1946 to help governments improve the health and education of children and their mothers

vaccinate to put a substance into the blood, using an injection, to protect a person from disease

vulnerable weak and easily hurt physically or emotionally

❯❯ FIND OUT MORE

Books

HIV/AIDS (Global Viewpoints), Noah Berlatsky, ed. (Greenhaven Press, 2011)

Hope in Hell: Inside the World of Médecins Sans Frontières, Dan Bortolotti (Firefly Books, 2010) (Suitable for older children and adults)

The International Red Cross (Global Organizations), Sean Connolly (Franklin Watts, 2010)

Malaria (Deadly Diseases and Epidemics), Bernard A. Marcus (Chelsea House Publishers, 2009)

The World Health Organization (Global Organizations), Sean Connolly (Franklin Watts, 2010)

Websites

Here are the websites of some of the organizations discussed in this book.

International Committee of the Red Cross:

www.icrc.org

Explains what the ICRC does, where it works, and includes publications.

International Federation of Red Cross and Red Crescent Societies:

www.ifrc.org

Explains what the IFRC does, where it works, and how to get involved. Includes publications.

Médecins Sans Frontières (MSF):

www.msf.org.uk

All about MSF's work around the world.

OneWorld Health:

www.oneworldhealth.org

About the drug development organization's activities around the world.

Save the Children:

www.savethechildren.org.uk

Explains the charity's work and how people can help.

Operation WellFound:

www.operationwellfound.org

Describes the work of this international water and sanitation charity.

World Health Organization:

www.who.int

The gateway to information on all of WHO's projects worldwide and its publication and statistics.

Visit these websites to find ways to become involved in healthcare charities:

Duke of Edinburgh's Award:

www.dofe.org

Red Cross:

www.redcross.org.uk

The Scout Association:

scouts.org.uk

St John Ambulance Cadets:

www.sja.org.uk/sja/young-people.aspx

TakingITGlobal:

www.tigweb.org

Online community with a mission to empower young people to understand and act on the world's greatest challenges.

Resources

Red Cross first aid teaching resources (for 11- to 16-year-olds)

www.redcross.org.uk/What-we-do/First-aid/First-aid-campaigns/Life-Live-it/ First-aid-in-schools-Life-Live-it/First-aid-education-kit-for-teachers

Topics to research

- Other charities and NGOs that help in emergencies.
- Healthcare charities working in your local area.
- Compare the healthcare needs in a MEDC with those in a LEDC.
- In-depth research into one of the healthcare charities discussed in this book.

INDEX